Stepping Stones

First lessons in
Accelerated Learning

for use with children aged 7-11

Eva Hoffman and Susan Norman

Illustrations by Justina Langley

Saffire PRESS

Acknowledgements

Our photographers were Martin Hoffman and Hugh L'Estrange. The models were: Sarah Hoffman, Jack Hoffman, Rachel Hoffman and Catherine L'Estrange.
Elaine Divine gave us the idea for this book in the first place.

Very many thanks to you all!

Mind mapping and integrated movements are key elements of Accelerated Learning. The relevant exercises in the book draw on the work of:
Tony Buzan, the originator of Mind Maps®, which is a Registered Trademark of the Buzan organisation, Poole, Dorset, UK, and
Paul Dennison, the originator of Brain Gym® a Registered Trademark of the Educational Kinesiology Foundation, Ventura Harbor Village, 1575 Spinaker Drive, Suite 204B, Ventura, California 930011, USA

First published January 2004

Published by   Saffire Press
               37 Park Hall Road
               East Finchley   Fax +44 (0)20 8444 0339
               London N2 9PT   books@saffirepress.co.uk
               England   www.saffirepress.co.uk

Design and layout: Hugh L'Estrange
Printed in Great Britain by Ashford Colour Press Ltd, Gosport, Hants, UK

ISBN 1 901564 09 6

Introduction

Stepping Stones is for everyone who wants to use an Accelerated Learning approach. It is for experienced, as well as new teachers, for Heads and teacher trainees – for everyone who wants to work with children in a more mind-and-heart-friendly way.

All you need to do is pick up the book and start.

Stepping Stones consists of 21 lesson plans at three progressive levels. They guide the teacher through seven core topics, explaining, developing and reinforcing the essential elements of Accelerated Learning:

- Building Self-Esteem
- Developing Emotional Intelligence
- Thinking creatively with Mind Mapping
- Moving to enhance Learning
- Discovering your Amazing Brain
- Maximising your Multiple Intelligences
- Using your Senses for Learning

The Accelerated Learning tools and techniques in this book augment and enhance existing teaching methods and the traditional curriculum. They also serve as a preparation for all areas of the school to be organised in a manner designed to reflect how children learn. As well as improving the children's ability to learn, Accelerated Learning promotes the personal growth and development of both teachers and learners.

As you work through the exercises you will notice a growing responsiveness and maturity in the children.

This is a book of tried and tested recipes for you to make your own.

Important recommendations for teachers experimenting with mind-friendly approaches:

- Before you give an exercise to children, DO IT YOURSELF!
- Children are the discoverers and what they discover is RIGHT.
- In these lessons spelling and other questions of accuracy do not matter. 'Editing' can come later.
- After every exercise encourage children to SHARE what they have learned with other children. It helps them to remember.
- Incorporate the learning from each lesson into subsequent lessons and activities.
- You are taking children on an exciting adventure of self-discovery so it has to be FUN.

STEP ONE

Lesson 1: *Good words, bad words*

Why do it? To make children aware of the effect of words
What you need Copies for each child of handouts 'Good/bad words' (p7),
  'Stepping Stones' (p10) and (two copies) 'I can't/I need help' (p9)
Time 'Good/bad words' 25 mins; 'I can' 20 mins; 'Stepping stones' 20 mins

Tell children that **good words** are the words that heal, empower, and make us feel happy and appreciated.

Bad words are the words that hurt, disempower, and make us feel miserable and not appreciated.

Most people use both good and bad words.

When other people talk to us using bad words, **they hurt us**.

When we use bad words when talking to others, **we hurt them**.

Draw two clouds on the board: a sunny good words cloud and a stormy bad words cloud.

Ask children: What sort of words do people say that make us feel good?

Write them in the cloud on the board.

Examples: *I like your smile. You (dance) really well. You're a good friend. You're really good at (drawing). Can you help me? I like it when you ...*

Ask children: What sort of words do people say that make us feel bad?

Write them in the cloud on the board.

Examples: *You're rubbish at (maths). Fatty. Stupid. Loser. You're lazy. You can't draw. I can't (sing).*

If children offer swear words, accept that they are bad words, but what we're looking for are things people say to us which make us feel bad.

Give children the 'Good/bad words' handout. Ask them to write words in the clouds which make them feel good and bad. They can write words from the board or words they think of themselves.

When they've finished ask them to share their words with a partner and look at their partner's words. If their partner has written something they think is really good, they can copy it into their own cloud.

Tell children: **Let's all try not to use the bad words. Let's try to use good words to one another so that we all feel good.**

I can

This activity can be done in a separate lesson.

Tell children that one of the expressions that can make us feel weak and helpless is **'I can't'**.

What can we say instead? When we want to delete something from the brain, we need to give it a substitute, something else to use instead. If we fail to do that, the old words jump back in.

Often when you say **'I can't'** you just mean **'I can't yet'**. Some time you will be able to do it. So at the moment, maybe you need some help. Maybe you need more practice. Or maybe you just need a bit more time.

So next time you start saying **'I can't'**, change it to:

'I need help.'

Or **'I need practice.'**

Or **'I need more time.'**

Give each child two copies of the picture (p9) to remind them what to say. When they've coloured them both in, laminate one for each child to use as a work mat at school. Give them one to take home to put on the wall or on the fridge. Their homework is to explain to their parents what they've learnt and to ask them to notice and correct every 'I can't'.

Stepping stones

This activity can be done in a separate lesson.

Tell children that it can take time to learn to be good at something new and learning often depends on the words you say to yourself.

Give each child a copy of the 'Stepping stones' picture (p10). Read (or ask them to read) the words each person is saying. Ask them which words are bad words to say to yourself when you are learning? Which words are good words to say to yourself?

Ask them to colour in the picture. They can decide which colours are best for which words.

Again they can take a copy of the picture home to show their parents what they're learning.

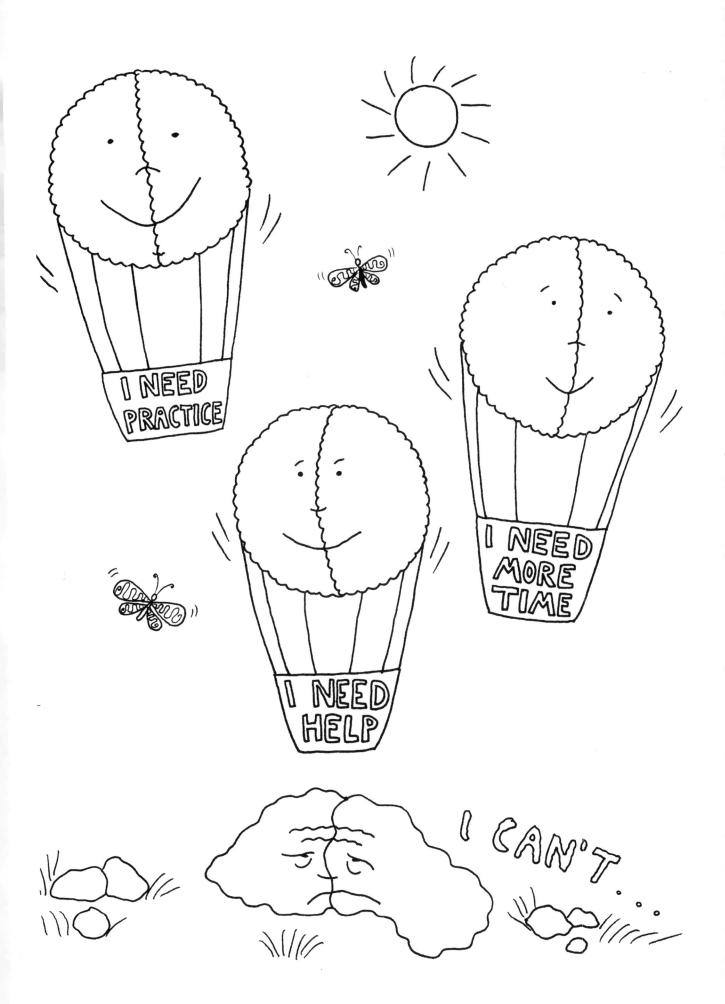

Developing Emotional Intelligence

Lesson 2: *Your inner weather report*

> ***Why do it?*** To make children more aware of how they feel, to validate their feelings, and to help them express their emotions in a safe way
>
> ***What you need*** Crayons/coloured pens/pencils/markers, drawing paper
>
> ***Time*** 30-45 minutes

Talk to children about their different feelings: joy, anger, love, sadness, anxiety, jealousy, empathy, excitement, etc. Tell children we all have good days and not so good days. Sometimes we feel content and calm and at other times anxious, nervous or angry.

All feelings are important.

It is good to know how we feel. But regardless of how we feel, we can control how we behave.

Ask children to sit up straight with both feet on the floor and then read the following words slowly and softly:

> *Close your eyes.*
> *Breathe slowly in… and out…*
> *and again in… and out…*
> *Put your hand on your heart*
> *and breathe again … in …*
> *out …*
> *Listen to your heart and let it*
> *tell you how you feel today.*
> *What is the weather like in your*
> *heart?*
> *Is it cloudy? … Is it sunny? …*
> *Is it raining? …*
> *Is there a storm? … Is it hot …*
> *or cold … or just nice and*
> *warm?*

Ask the children to draw a picture of what the weather feels like in their hearts.

When they've finished, ask them to think about what the different types of weather might mean. If it's raining, is it happy rain or sad rain? Remember, different people respond to different types of weather differently. Ducks and plants like wet weather. Most people like sunshine, but not when it's too hot. Ask for suggestions about the different feelings that each sort of weather might represent. All answers are correct.

Use this as an opportunity to check feeling words the children know and introduce one or two new ones:

happy • sad • excited • anxious • tired • comfortable • content • strong • powerful • depressed • unsettled • thrilled

Ask them to explain their picture to someone else, saying what their weather means to them.

Alternatives

If you do this activity again, you might give children the chance to express their feelings in different ways, eg through mime, making an animal puppet or a mask, dancing, or writing a poem or a metaphor. When children have expressed their feelings artistically, encourage them afterwards to share with their friends or one other person what they feel and how they express their emotions.

If some children do not want to talk about their feelings, respect their wish for privacy. They can still join in the activity by choosing some weather they would like to illustrate and talking about their picture. Maybe next time they will be more comfortable and want to share.

If children draw pictures which alert you to the fact that they might have deeper emotional problems or be seriously depressed, find a moment to talk to them yourself in private. If you do not feel you have the skill or experience, then find someone who has.

It is often easier to talk about your feelings, particularly if you aren't used to it, if they are one step removed, eg talking about the weather, describing how your doll or your puppet or your pet is feeling.

Thinking creatively with Mind Mapping

Lesson 3: *Making radiant associations*

Why do it? To introduce mind mapping by encouraging creative trains of thought

What you need A whiteboard or an OHP and at least four different coloured markers, blank sheets of A3 or A4 paper and at least four different coloured pens for each child or (for younger children) copies of the 'Dotty mind map' (p15)

Time 30 minutes

Give all the children a sheet of paper (or a copy of the 'Dotty mind map' which will help them orientate their drawing on the page). As you produce your mind map on the OHP or white board, ask them to draw the same thing on their paper.

In the middle of a landscape sheet draw a light bulb (anything you think children will like drawing).

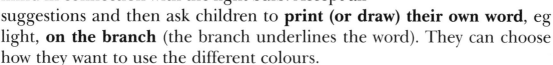

Coming out of the central picture draw a thick branch. Ask children to think what first comes to mind in connection with the light bulb. Accept all suggestions and then ask children to **print (or draw) their own word**, eg light, **on the branch** (the branch underlines the word). They can choose how they want to use the different colours.

Draw three more branches. Ask children to write (or draw) on each branch another word that comes to mind when you think about the centre picture (light bulb), eg glass, electricity, useful.

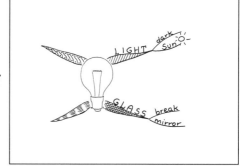

Now draw two thin branches coming out of every thick branch and on them write (draw) what comes to your mind when you think about the word on the thick branch. From light you might get bright, dark, heavy, shining. From glass you might get break, sharp, drinking, etc.

If children can't immediately think of a word to go on any line, they leave it blank. An idea may come to them later.

Thinking creatively with Mind Mapping

When everyone has finished, they share their mind maps with two or more different partners. Ask them to count how many words on their mind map are the same as the other person's and how many are different.

Give children the opportunity to write words and/or draw pictures on any blank lines to complete their mind map if they wish.

Explain that because no two brains are identical, no two pictures or mind maps will be exactly the same either. Celebrate the fact that all of us **are all different, unique and special.**

- Everything that comes to children's minds is correct. Refrain from looking for logic and explanations. The associations need to be absolutely free: flowing freely, and free from pressure, free from expectations and free of judgement.
- Do not expect accuracy. Just for the time being spelling does not matter. We want nothing to stop the flow of ideas.
- Any stimulus can give rise to numerous different ideas, any of which can be developed.

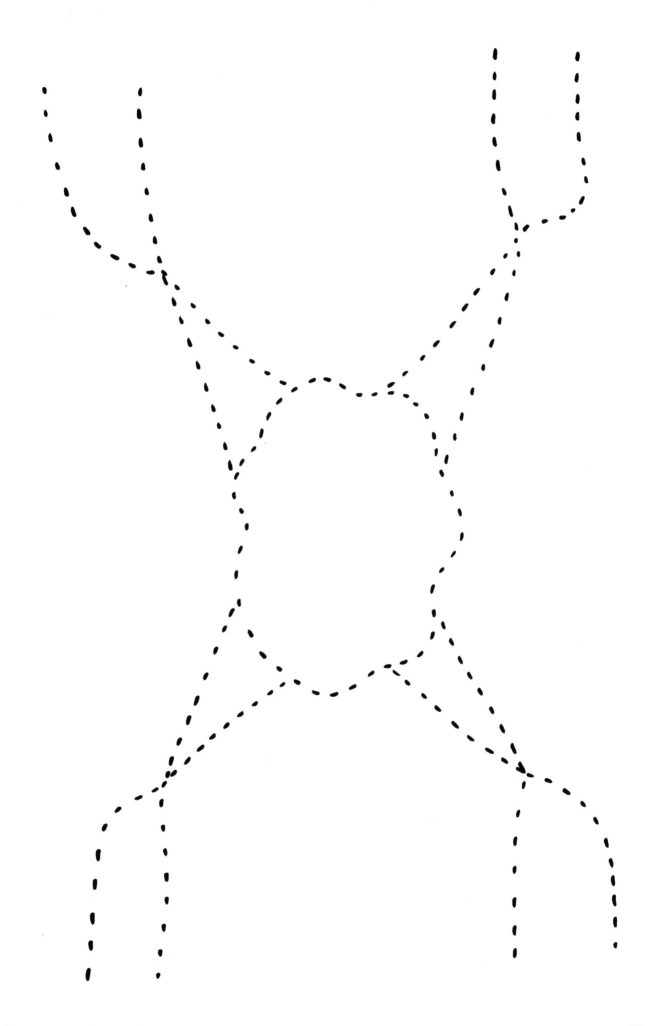

Lesson 4: *Cross-patting*

> ***Why do it?*** To integrate the brain (connect the left and right hemisphere)
> ***What you need*** Space for children to move, drinking water
> ***Time*** 5-10 minutes

Encourage children to have a drink of water before they do exercises. Electrolytes in water improve the brain functioning.

Standing (older children)

- Tell children to stand up straight and imagine a coloured string going vertically from their nose to their feet. When they do the movements, their hands must cross this line.
- Ask them to put their right arm out and then pat their left shoulder three times. Ask them: *'Did your arm cross the line?'* Then they put their left arm out and pat their right shoulder three times.
- They can now pat their opposite sides (at chest level), left side with the right hand and then right side with the left hand, … then hips … and thighs … and finally …
- Ask them to lift their left leg and pat their left knee with their right hand three times and then to lift their right leg and pat their right knee with their left hand three times.
- Repeat the last movement several times, alternately touching opposite hand to opposite knee.
- They can also touch their elbow to the opposite knee.

16

Moving to enhance Learning

Children tend to do the movements quite quickly – and it is fine to do them quickly sometimes as a warm up. However the exercise is most effective when it is done as slowly as possible. Say to the children: This is good. Now **who can do it really slowly?**

Until it becomes automatic, keep asking children, **'Is your hand crossing your imaginary line?'** And **remind them to breathe**. (People often hold their breath when doing exercises, which is definitely not good for the brain!)

Sitting (younger children)

Cross-patting is easier when sitting than standing, so encourage young children and those with balance difficulties to sit while doing the exercise.

Stickers

When working with very young children, stick a red sticker to each child's right hand and left knee, and a green sticker to their left hands and right knees. **Red meets red and green meets green** when cross-patting.

Do cross-patting whenever children have been sitting still for more than 20 minutes – or at the beginning of a lesson to get them into a good state for learning.

All movement is good for the body and good for the brain. It stimulates the blood flow, builds our bones, and strengthens our muscles.

There is a special kind of movement, 'integrated movement', that actually helps the brain work better.

The right hemisphere of the brain controls the movements on the left side of the body and vice versa. Movements such as cross-patting which activate alternate opposite sides of the body with the arms and/or legs crossing the midline stimulate interaction between the different parts of the brain. Marching while swinging the arms across the centre of the body is also effective.

When we are under stress, even mild stress, different parts of the brain do not communicate well and coherent thinking becomes difficult if not impossible.

Integrated movement:

• reconnects different parts of the brain and maintains existing connections

• creates new connections between the brain cells

People don't learn well when their brains are not integrated. Doing integrated movements (also known as Brain Gym®) has the potential to help them learn.

Discovering your Amazing Brain

Lesson 5: *Brain likes and dislikes*

> ***Why do it?*** To begin making children aware of the way their brains work
> ***What you need*** A copy for each child of the 'Brain likes/dislikes' sheet (p21) and coloured pens/markers
> ***Time*** 30-45 minutes

Ask children to make fists of their hands and to put them together. Tell them that this is how big their brains are.

Tell them that their brains are incredibly brilliant and they need to be treated well if we want them to work well.

There are some things which are good for the brain and others which can stop the brain from working well.

Give each child a copy of the 'Brain likes/dislikes' sheet and some coloured markers. Ask children to write **on the dotted lines** of a 'happy brain' what they think is good for their brains.

Make a copy of the happy brain on the board and ask children to tell you what they have written. Write up their suggestions. Add in ideas they don't know, eg that fish oil is very good for the brain.

Ask them to take a different colour marker and write on the continuous lines the things they hadn't originally thought of.

Make sure children have the most important words written down.

Repeat the process with the dislikes.

Good things for the brain
Oxygen, water, fish oils, vegetables, interest, relaxed alertness, sleep, integrated movement, fun, challenge, laughter, smiles

Bad things for the brain
Stress, lack of oxygen, water, sleep, movement, poor nutrition, a lot of sugar, food additives, boredom.

Studies have shown an almost immediate improvement in attention and test scores when children have taken fish oil supplements – and similar results when children have avoided food additives, particularly the 'E' preservatives (especially artificial colouring).

Shouts

Ask the children to stand up and look at one of the words they've written on the continuous lines of the happy brain (the things they didn't think of themselves and which are new to them). On the count of three, everyone shouts out, all together with a big smile,
'Brains like ...' (the word on that line).

Do the same with the dislikes, but this time children try to look and sound as miserable as possible.

Repeat the like and dislike 'shouts' for as long as there are words to be shouted. Some children may drop out as they have no more words, but they can still 'act' happy or sad.

It is important to do some kind of activity with the words children didn't previously know (eg write them in a different colour and shout them out), otherwise they just tend to remember the things they knew originally.

Lights

Put on all the lights in the room and draw the curtains if possible.

Tell children: When you are relaxed but alert, your brains work well. We can say that there's a light on in your brains. However, when you are under stress, when you are angry, anxious or worried, your brain shuts down. It is as if the light in your brain has gone off and there is darkness.'

Switch off the light.

Now you understand a bit about the brain, we're going to learn different ways of 'switching on the light' (switch on the light) in your brain again so that it can work well again. You already know one way! (Cross-patting.)

Other ways to reconnect brains are: **Sleeping Eights** (p37), **Crossed wrists and ankles** (p57) and **Brain buttons** (p59).

Stepping Stones ©*Eva Hoffman and Susan Norman 2004*

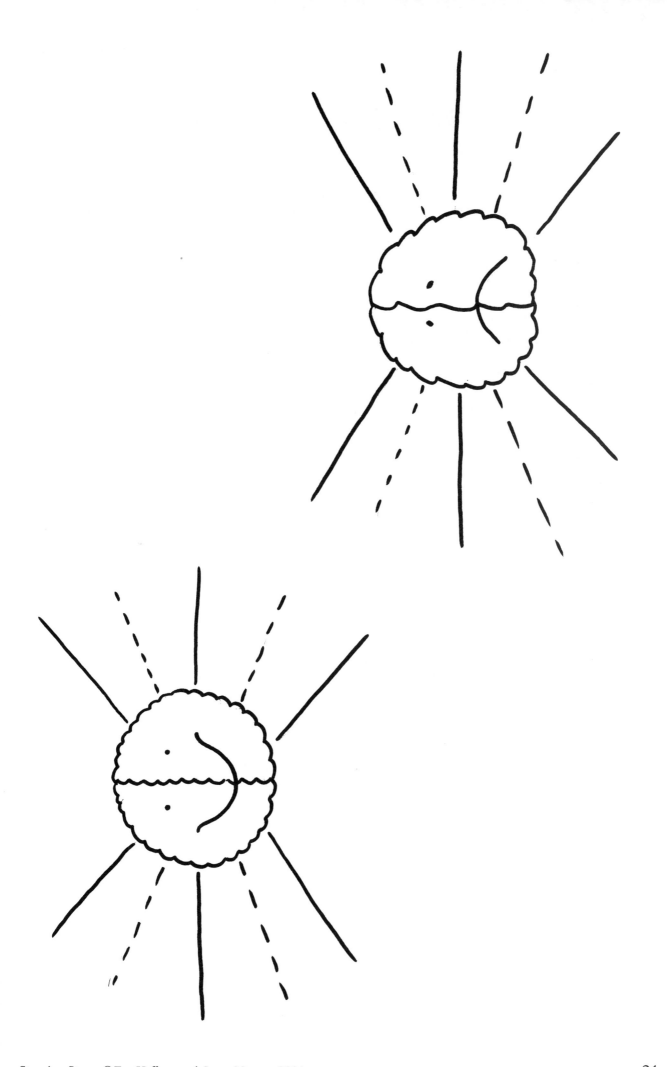

Lesson 6: *We are all intelligent*

> *Why do it?* To make children aware of the fact that they have many different intelligences, all of which are important and valued.
>
> *What you need* Coloured pens and one copy of 'Intelligences mind map' (p24) for each child (or blank paper)
>
> *Time* 30-45 minutes

Tell children: **You are intelligent.** It is most likely that you are intelligent in a different way from your sister, your brother, your parents or your friend, but you are intelligent.

Your intelligences are your strengths, the things you are good at, the things you like doing.

What is more, **your intelligences can get even better if you work to improve them.**

Give each child a copy of the 'Intelligences mind map', or draw it on the board for children to copy. Each arm of the star in the picture represents one intelligence, one kind of strength. Talk about each branch and discuss with children people they know who are strong in this intelligence, eg for music, the music teacher, Madonna, one of the children in the class who can play an instrument or sing well.

When you have completed all the nine branches on the mind map, ask children: Which is your best intelligence, your greatest strength? Colour it in your favourite colour. Can you find another one and colour it in your second favourite colour? And another one?

On the thin lines ask them to write the names of people who are strong in this intelligence. They may think of celebrities, TV personalities, book characters, members of their family, and, of course, themselves.

Ask children to share their completed mind maps with two other children and see what their strengths are and whose names they have written.

Isn't it interesting how different we are?

Maximising your Multiple Intelligences

Examples of people with different strengths (intelligences)

Music	Wolfgang Amadeus Mozart, Robbie Williams
Picture	Pablo Picasso, LS Lowry, Christopher Wren, Rolf Harris
Practical	Charlie Dimmock, Jamie Oliver, 'Changing Room' team, the school caretaker
Words	William Shakespeare, JK Rowling, Roald Dahl
Nature	Charles Darwin, David Attenborough, Alan Titchmarsh
Number	Isaac Newton, Bill Gates, Carol Vorderman
People	Princess Diana, Mother Teresa
Body	David Beckham, Riverside Dancers
Self	Martin Luther King, Nelson Mandela
(Spiritual	Mahatma Gandhi)

Intelligent actions

Organise the children into nine groups, each representing one of the intelligences. Give them five minutes to devise and practise a group action (or actions) to demonstrate 'their' intelligence. Everyone then watches each group 'perform' – and copies the action/s of that group.

One of the great values of the Multiple Intelligences theory is that individuals are valued for all their strengths, rather than being judged simply on their IQ. It is a way of raising self-esteem. Therefore it is important to respect how children feel about themselves and acknowledge everything they want to claim about their own abilities without judgement.

The seven intelligences first proposed by Howard Gardner in his book *Frames of Mind* were Verbal/Linguistic, Mathematical/Logical, Visual/Spatial, Musical, Bodily/Kinesthetic, Inter-personal (awareness of others) and Intra-personal (knowledge of self). These last two, he linked together as the 'personal intelligences', and they are the basis of Emotional intelligence as proposed by Daniel Goleman in his book of that name. Gardner later added an eighth intelligence, Naturalist, and he is also talking about Existential intelligence, which some people call Spiritual intelligence.

We have used simpler words for children, and although we also acknowledge a spiritual intelligence, we have not included it in the mind map so as not to force it on teachers.

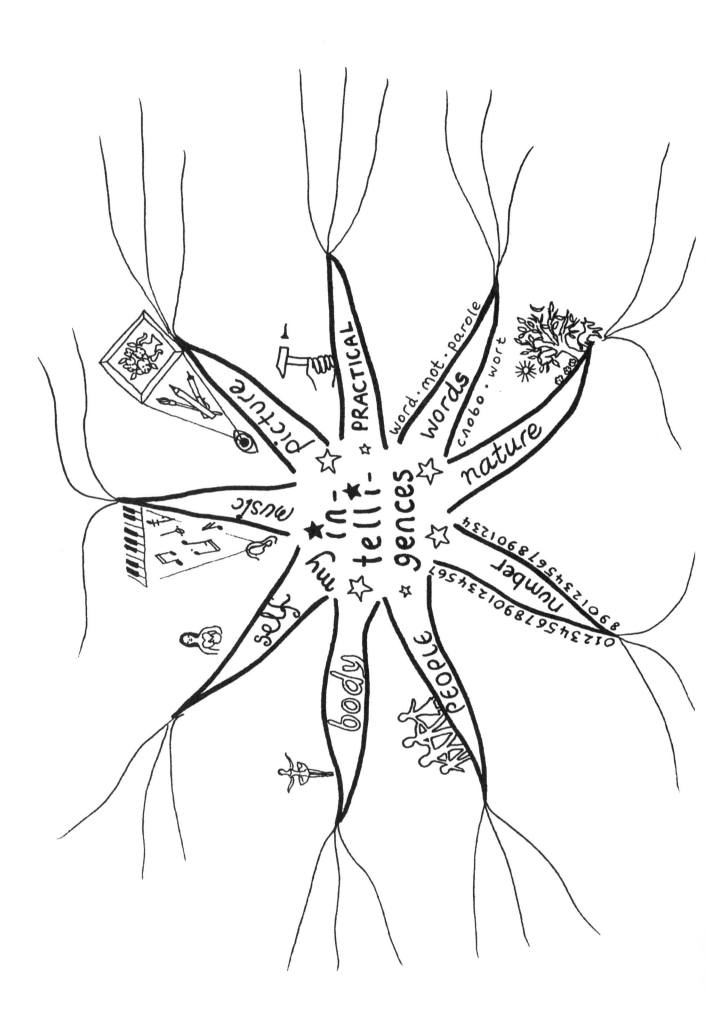

Using your Senses for Learning

Lesson 7: *Blindfolds and earplugs*

Why do it? To bring to children's awareness the role senses play in everyday life before we look at the role they play in learning.

What you need Blindfolds for half the class, earplugs (or cotton wool) for each child, about 30 objects (could be in 'feely bags')

Time 20-45 minutes

Ask children: How do you know that I am standing in front of you? (They can see.) Tell them: Close your eyes and keep them closed.

Go to the back of the room and ask: 'Now how do you know where I am standing? (They can hear your voice – maybe they felt you walk past.)

How do you know that you are sitting? (They can feel their bodies touching the chair, their feet touching the floor.)

Is it warm here or chilly? How do you know that? (Feeling on their skin.)

(You might also bring in some sprigs of mint, some strong smelling flowers, 'smelly' non-toxic pens, or anything else with a strong smell for children to experience the sense of smell. And chocolate and apples are always popular for experiencing the sense of taste.)

Your senses give you all the information about the world around you.

Everything you learn starts with your senses.

Sight

Demonstrate the activity first with a volunteer who you blindfold. Give the child one of the objects from the feely bag. As well as asking them to guess what it is, encourage the class to suggest other things the child can say about the object …

Is it big or small? Hard or soft? Long or short? Wet or dry? Soft or smooth?

Ask children to work with a partner. Blindfold one of each pair.

Suggestions for 'feely bag' objects

eraser • pencil sharpener • coloured pencil/crayon • plastic teaspoon • plastic fork • tealight or birthday candle • conker • carrot • potato • heart cut out of yellow or blue velvet • large paper clip • zip fastener • cotton reel • hair 'scrunchy' • ribbon • child's plastic letter of the alphabet • triangle cut out of sandpaper • small roll of sellotape • button • small ruler • 2p coin • credit card (expired!) • wrapped sweet • small paint brush • hard-boiled egg • photograph • empty water bottle • tissue/pack of tissues • bottle top • calculator • CD or CD-ROM

Give two or three objects from the feely bag to every pair and let them work together: one describing as much as they can about the object and the other putting objects in the blindfolded child's hands and prompting.

Do the activity a second time with the other child in each pair wearing the blindfold. Give each pair new objects.

When the blindfold comes off, ask the children to write down everything they have found out about the objects without using their eyes. Which things couldn't they know? (colours, flat designs, words, kind of discs – CDs or CD-ROMs.)

Suggestions for contents of feely bag

Blindfolds again

Take children to the hall or outside if the weather is right, and blindfold one child in each pair.

Tell the children without blindfolds that they are responsible for the blindfolded children's safety.

Let children experience using their ears and sense of touch in the context of an open space. After a while, let the children swap roles.

Afterwards, ask them to tell others and you about what happened. What did they experience? How did they feel? What couldn't they know without their eyes? Which senses did they have to use? Did they like it or not? Did they find it difficult or easy?

Earplugs

Encourage a few children (or all children, possibly at different times) to put earplugs (or cotton wool) in their ears.

Describe something or show a video and then ask the children to describe their experience of being deprived of their hearing.

Remind children not to put small objects in their ears and not to try this activity without an adult present.

STEP TWO

Lesson 8: *Mistake monsters*

> *Why do it?* To help children view mistakes as a necessary part of learning and to realise that everyone makes mistakes
>
> *What you need* Blank paper and coloured pens/markers
>
> *Time* 30 minutes

Ask children: Did you know that in order **to learn anything you MUST make mistakes?** Isn't it strange that everybody makes mistakes and yet mistakes make so many people angry, upset or embarrassed?

Mistakes are to teach you, not to embarrass you.

Ask children how many of them have baby brothers or sisters or cousins – or if they know any babies. How do babies learn to walk? Do they just stand up and start walking? How many times do you think they fall over? What do their mummies and daddies say to them?

What do they say? 'You stupid baby. Can't you even walk yet? Oh no, don't tell me you've fallen over again! Come on. Walk quicker! You're a very slow walker.' Or do they say 'Well done! What a clever baby. That's right. Let me help you. Come to me.'

It's the same with everything we learn. In the beginning we make mistakes with reading and writing and sums and drawing and dancing and football – everything. How do we get better? We try again and keep practising, and then we notice that we're not making so many mistakes and things seem to get easier.

What are all the things you can do now that you couldn't do when you were born? (Blow your nose, clean your teeth, dress yourself, walk, talk, read, write, run, kick a ball, catch a ball, crawl, sing, etc.) And next year you'll probably be able to do lots of those things even better – and lots of new things too. And while you're learning each thing, you need to experiment and try – and sometimes what you do won't be perfect and so we call it a mistake.

So if mistakes are our friends, let's make friends with them.

Building Self–Esteem

Draw a picture representing a mistake, for example, a funny monster or anything else you want. These are my mistake monsters (show children the pictures from this page, or reproduce them on the board).

When they've drawn their pictures, tell them that your monsters have silly names. One is called Squeak (which is the sound it makes) and the other one is Assa Drassa. Whenever you make a mistake, you just say, 'Oh Squeak', and laugh. Or 'Oh Assa Drassa! Thank you for helping me learn.'

Tell them: Think of a funny sound-name for your mistake monster. Something that will make you laugh. Write the word under your picture and remember to say it every time you make a mistake.

Remember, that **the more relaxed you are, the better you will learn.**

You might like to make a couple of obvious mistakes in the next 15 minutes so you can speak to 'your' mistake monsters.

Lesson 9: *Letting go of labels*

> *Why do it?* To make children aware of the power labels have and the harm they cause
>
> *What you need* A photocopy of each handout for each child, 'Words that hurt' (p32), 'A day without labels' (p33)
>
> *Time* Letting go 30 mins, Labelling actions 20 mins, Armour 20 mins

Tell children: **Labels make no sense. No person is**
- **always horrible or always sweet,**
- **always honest or always a liar,**
- **always lazy or always hard-working**
- **always anything!**

Ask children to remember the words they wrote in their 'Words that hurt' clouds (Lesson 1, p6). How do they feel when people use these words to them? Do they like it or not like it? Does it make them feel happy and strong or sad and weak? Does it make them angry?

Ask them whether they have ever used hurtful words to other people. Most of us have at some time or another, even if we now feel sorry about it. How do they think the other person felt when they heard the hurtful words?

Give children the 'Words that hurt' handout and ask them to write examples of the words other people have used which hurt them. Then ask them to write the words they have used in the past which they think may have hurt other people – even if they're sorry now.

> Children are usually much better at finding words that have hurt them than they are at finding words they have used. You can take off the pressure by using the past tense (words you used in the past when you didn't know better) or by saying 'even if you're sorry now'. If children do not admit to using hurtful words (even if you know they have), don't force them. This activity is about raising awareness, not about naming and shaming!

Developing Emotional Intelligence

Labelling actions not people

If you think the children are old enough, you can tell them that instead of labelling a person we may want to label their actions.

For example, say: *You haven't done the work.* Don't say: *You are lazy.*

Say: *That answer was wrong.* Don't say: *You're rubbish at maths.*

Give them some more examples of things to say or not to say and ask them what to say instead, eg

Say: *You did a stupid thing.* What don't you say? (You are stupid.)

Say: *You lost the game.* What don't you say? (You're a loser.)

Say: *You have done a horrid thing.* What don't you say? (You are horrid.)

Labelling a person indicates that you think they will not change. Labelling a person's actions shows them that they have a choice about how to behave. They can choose to do something different next time.

A day without labels

Give children the 'Day without labels' handout. Ask them to colour it in.

Together with children decide which day will be their first day when nobody labels anybody, when all 'name-calling' is banned.

Put their posters on the walls to remind children about label-free days.

Label-proof armour

This activity can be done in another lesson.

Tell children: Although we won't use labels in this class, there may be people outside this class who will call us names, tease us and give us horrid labels. We need to learn how to defend ourselves.

You can put on 'label-proof armour'! It will not let any nasty words get to you and hurt you! All you need to do is to use your powerful imagination to keep you safe!

Tell children: Draw a picture of yourself and then draw bubble-armour all around you so that when people 'throw' nasty words at you, they will just bounce off. Make your armour the best colour to protect you.

Show children the picture from this page to give them the idea.

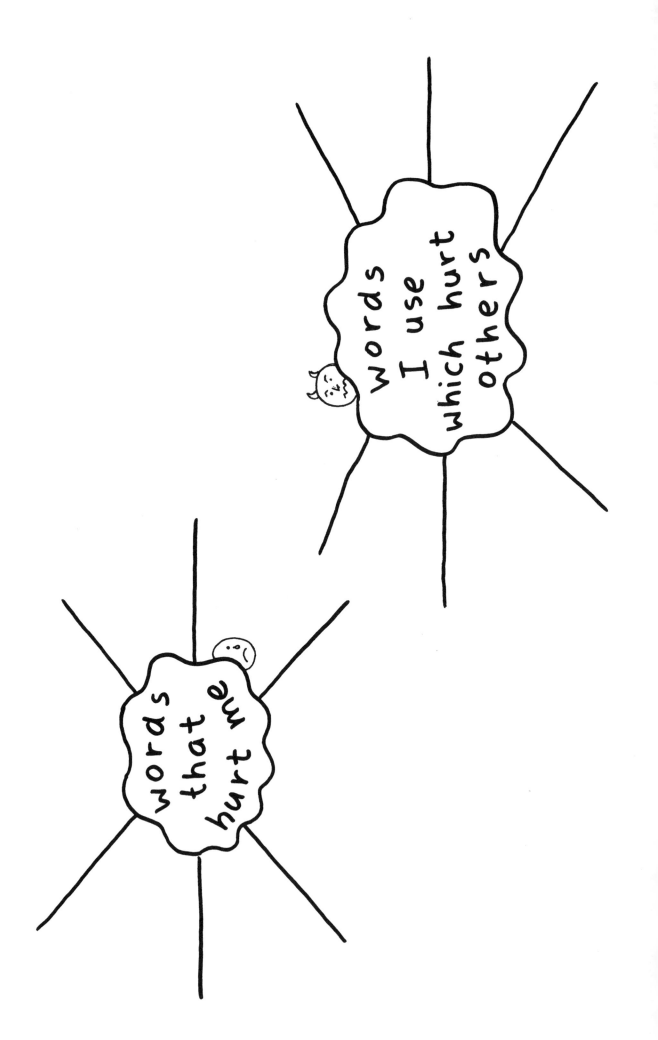

A day without Labels

TODAY

Lesson 10: *Key words in Mind Mapping*

Why do it? To learn to identify key words, one of the essential elements of mind mapping

What you need Coloured pens and possibly a photocopy of the blank 'Cat' mind map (p37), and/or a blank sheet of paper, and/or a 'Dotty mind map' (p15)

Time 30 minutes

Draw a cat with four mind map branches on the board.

Ask children to suggest sentences to describe the cat – and write the sentences on the lines. Examples:

My cat is black.

Her name is Smoky.

She has got four kittens.

She is cheeky.

Help children find the key words in each sentence.

My cat is black. You don't need the word 'cat' because you've got the picture. Key word: **black**.

Her name is Smoky. We probably need both the words **name** and **Smoky**.

She has got four kittens. We probably need both **kittens** and **four**.

She is cheeky. Key word: **cheeky**.

Tell children: When we're drawing a mind map we only use the key words and we only write one word on each line. If you want to give more information, you put it on thinner lines coming off the big branch.

Black is part of the cat's physical appearance. So the main branch says 'appearance' and the thinner branch says 'black'.

Second branch is 'name', with 'Smoky' on a thinner line.

Third branch is 'kittens', with 'four' on a thinner line.

Fourth branch is 'personality', with 'cheeky' on a thinner line.

Ask children to copy the completed mind map.

Thinking creatively with Mind Mapping

Then ask them to add some extra words (possibly with guidance from you) to describe her **personality** (which they add on thinner lines coming off the main branch) and **appearance** (eg add a line coming from the main branch which says 'paws' and a small line coming off that for the word 'white'.) They might also write in the names and colours of the kittens.

The number of lines coming off branches depends on how much information you have about each aspect. Every mind map will be different.

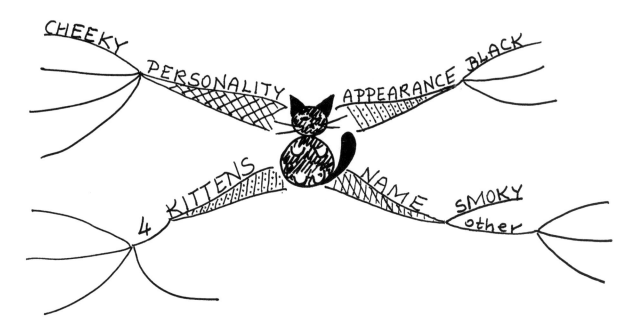

New mind map

Ask older children to think of another animal – it could be their own pet or an animal they know about from books or from a visit to the zoo – and write four sentences about it. (Help them think about new things they could describe, eg the speed it moves or the sound it makes.) Then they circle the key words in each sentence.

Give each child a piece of blank paper or the 'Dotty mind map' (p15) to help them orientate themselves on the page. While they are drawing a picture of the animal in the centre, go round and check which key words they have circled and give help as necessary.

Ask them to produce their mind map about the animal.

Encourage children to explain their mind maps to one another.

Moving to enhance Learning

Lesson 11: *Sleeping Eights & Butterflies (and Dots and Streamers)*

> ***Why do it?*** To integrate the left and right hemispheres, to exercise the eyes and to improve hand-eye co-ordination
>
> ***What you need*** Blank paper and coloured markers for Sleeping Eights (or dotty handout p40), coloured sticky dots for Dots, photocopies of the butterfly sheet (p41) for Butterflies, crepe paper for Streamers
>
> ***Time*** 10 mins for Sleeping Eights or Dots, 30 mins for Butterflies, 5 mins for Streamers (plus preparation time)

Sleeping Eights

Sleeping Eights can be a challenge of co-ordination for many children, so we offer several ways of doing it, so that those who really need it can get enough practice.

- Encourage children to drink water before they do exercises.
- Give children coloured markers and a copy of the dotted Sleeping Eight handout (p40).
- Tell them to turn the sheet on its side (landscape style).
- Ask them to start at the centre and join the dots. It is important to follow the arrows – up to the left and then round and back to the centre (like the start of the small letter 'a'), then up following the arrow and round to the right, coming back to the centre so that you have drawn a 'figure of eight' lying on its side.
- Tell the children to continue drawing over the Sleeping Eight in a flowing movement until you tell them to stop.

Look round to see that they're doing it correctly. Make sure that their hands are going upwards in the middle and downwards on the outside of each loop. If some children are making the Sleeping Eights very small emcourage them to make them larger and larger. If others are making them large ask them to try making them smaller and smaller.

> The following activities transfer the Sleeping Eights movement from paper to the air. You can do any of them immediately or in a future lesson. Older children can probably do it without aids, but coloured dots and butterflies make the activity easier for younger children. Streamers are fun for all.

Dots and Butterflies

The basic activity is to make a fist with your thumb sticking up, hold it out at arm's length in front of you as you draw a Sleeping Eight in the air, making sure that

- the midpoint you start from is in line with your nose (so that the hand crosses the body's midline)
- you always start the loops moving upwards from the centre
- you keep your head still
- you follow the movement of your thumb with your eyes.

Do the movement several times, first with one thumb, then with the other thumb, then with hands clasped together. Make the movement as big as you can.

Try the activity for yourself any time you're feeling a bit tired and see how much more refreshed you feel.

With younger children, you can help them follow their thumb with their eyes by putting a coloured dot on their thumbnail.

Alternatively, make as many photocopies of the sheet of butterflies (p41) as you need for each child to have one (or two). Children colour in their butterfly/butterflies. Some children might prefer to have a pattern already sketched in, and others may prefer 'blank' wings for them to draw their own pattern. The butterflies need to be cut out – either by you or by the children.

Stick butterflies to children's thumbs with sticky tape.

Streamers

You may like to make (or get children to make) coloured streamers by taking blocks of crepe paper in different colours (in the folded form in which you buy it) and cutting a 3 cm strip from the end. When it's unfolded, it becomes a streamer.

Moving to enhance Learning

Then holding a coloured streamer, all the children stand up and do Sleeping Eights. Remember to get them going up from the centre and crossing the midline of the body.

If you are short of space, have half the class doing the activity while the others applaud – and then swap over.

Enjoy the effect! It's fun to see.

Many people draw one loop bigger than the other, so encourage children to make their loops the same size if they can – although they may be unable to see the difference in size. If children's brains are not yet fully integrated, you may find that they are unable to draw Sleeping Eights unaided. Without putting any pressure on them to succeed, make a game of it and hold their hand to help them make the shape in the correct way

If children are not doing the activity correctly, it is almost certainly because it is beyond their physical and developmental ability, and not because they are being naughty. (You will be able to recognise if any child is 'being naughty' to cover up their embarrassment if they feel there is pressure to succeed.) Ask them to remember their mistake monster (p28) and just say its sound-name, and remind them of their posters: 'I need more time' (p9) and 'Stepping stones' (p10). Assure them that with more practice, they will be able to do it.

Sleeping Eights

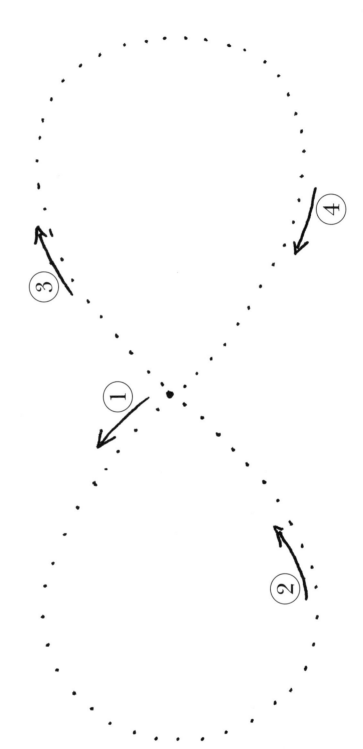

Lesson 12: *Three brains in one*

> **Why do it?** To make children aware of the functions of the three parts of the
> brain and show them how stress and strong emotions make thinking and
> learning very slow or even impossible
>
> **What you need** A copy of the 'Three brains in one' handout (p44) for each
> child
>
> **Time** 30 minutes

Ask for two volunteers to help you describe the parts of the brain.

Tell children that the part of the brain which is responsible for your survival (heartbeat, breathing, digestion, reflexes) is the REPTILIAN BRAIN, the most primitive part of the brain. This is the part that developed first.

Your first volunteer makes a fist and holds his hand up straight.

The part of the brain which developed next was the LIMBIC SYSTEM, also called the mammalian brain. (Mammals developed after reptiles.) The limbic system is the seat of your emotions, of your immune system (defence against disease) and of your long-term memory.

Your volunteer puts his other hand over the top of the fist.

The third part of the brain is called the NEO-CORTEX, your thinking brain. It solves problems and creates ideas. This is divided into two parts (the left and right hemispheres) which link together in the centre.

Your second volunteer links her fingers together and puts them over the other child's hands.

Explain that our reptilian brain is in charge of our bodies' needs: for food, water, being not too cold and not too hot, needing to go to the toilet. If these things are not OK, the reptilian brain blocks your thinking brain.

If your reptilian brain is OK, then your limbic system, your emotional brain, is the next gateway. When you experience strong emotions, such as sadness or fear or stress, your limbic system stops you thinking clearly.

Only when your reptilian brain and your limbic system are OK can you think and learn properly with the neo-cortex, the thinking brain.

Discovering your Amazing Brain

Handy brains

This activity is more suitable for older children.

Help children remember the three parts of the brain by asking them to work in pairs and use their hands to create their own models of the brain.

Call out **reptilian brain** – and everyone holds up one fist to show the reptilian brain. Remind them that this is their survival brain.

Call out **limbic system**. Everyone demonstrates the limbic brain with two hands and you remind them that it's the emotional brain.

Call out **survival brain** and make sure everyone recreates the reptilian brain with one fist.

Neo-cortex. (They have to work with their partner.)

Emotional brain – Limbic system

Thinking brain – Neo-cortex

Keep calling out the six permutations until you think the class have remembered them.

Diagram

Give each child a copy of the 'Three brains in one' handout (p44). Help them fill in the key with the words 'neo-cortex', 'limbic system' and 'reptilian brain'. Tell them to write the functions of the different parts in the clouds. (Survival brain, emotional brain, thinking brain.)

Then ask them to number the three parts of the brain according to the order in which they developed and in which they act as gateways.

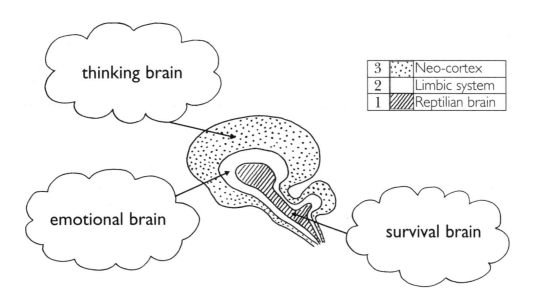

3		Neo-cortex
2		Limbic system
1		Reptilian brain

Three brains in one

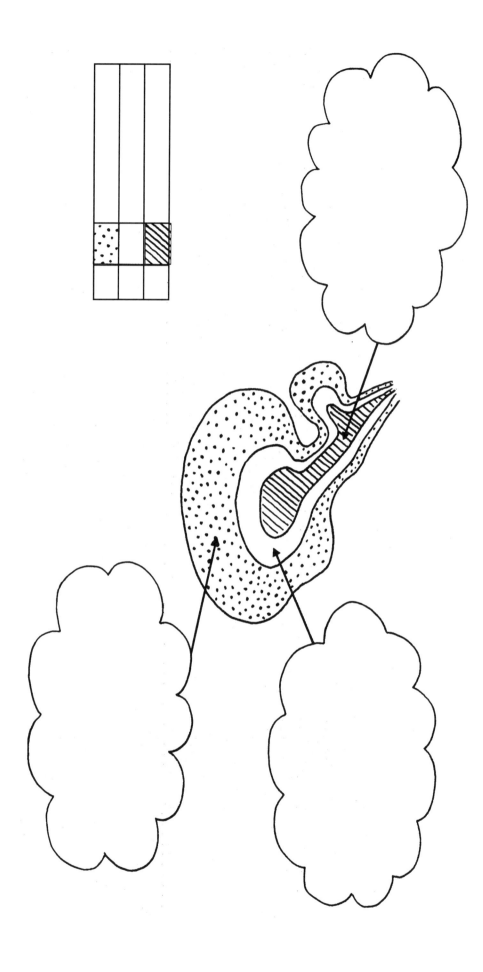

Maximising your Multiple Intelligences

Lesson 13: *Your strengths*

Why do it? To encourage children to recognise and appreciate their strengths and the strengths of others

What you need An A3 copy of the 'Intelligences' mind map for each child (make A3 photocopies of p46), OHP or whiteboard

Time 30-45 minutes

Draw a mind map on the board showing the thick branches with the nine intelligences in the same configuration as the children's copy.

Give each child a copy of the 'Intelligences' mind map.

Starting with **music**, ask children if they like singing, listening to music or tapping rhythms. Ask them to underline the things they like in the colour of their choice.

Talk the children round the whole mind map, explaining words as necessary and making sure they are all following. The importance of this activity is to enhance children's self-awareness and self-esteem. Let children mark whatever they want. Avoid making corrections or comments at this stage.

When you have been all round the mind map, ask children to find their two or three very best intelligences and colour in all the associated pictures and the main branch with colours of their choice.

Ask children to share and compare their mind maps with two or three other children. Tell them that the fact we are different makes the world a truly interesting place.

Draw the intelligences in a different order each time you do a new mind map to convey the message that no intelligence is more important than any other.

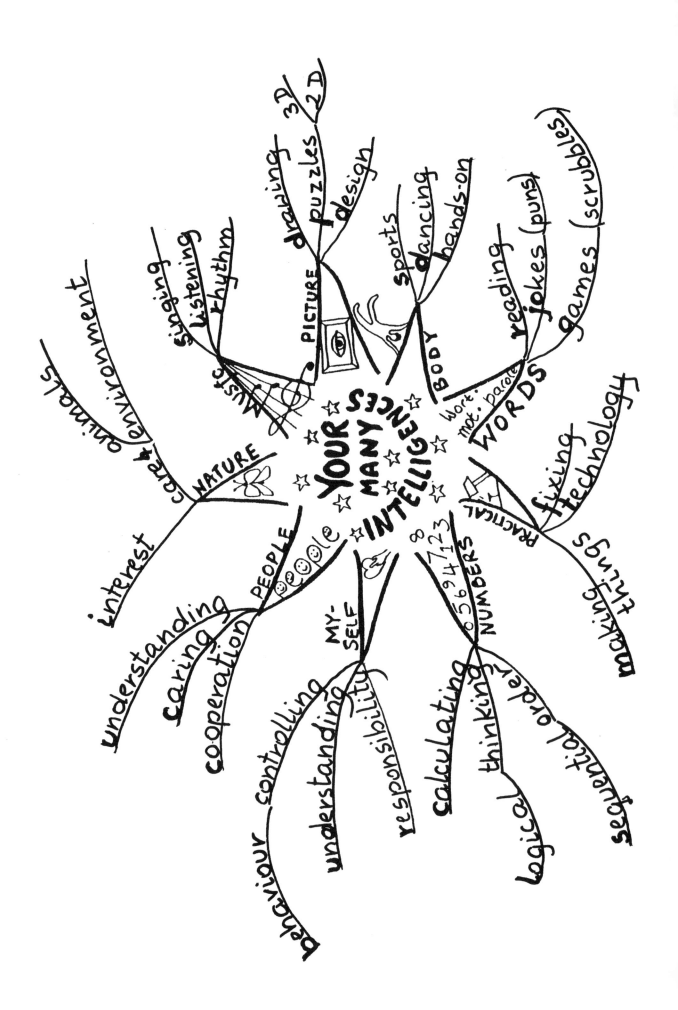

Using your Senses for Learning

Lesson 14: *Learning starts with the senses*

> ***Why do it?*** To help children recognise the role senses play in their learning
>
> ***What you need*** An OHP or a whiteboard and coloured markers; one copy of the 'Senses' handout (p48) for each child
>
> ***Time*** 30 minutes

Draw a version of the senses mind map on the board.

Ask children: **What have you learned that you couldn't have learned without using our eyes?** (eg colours)

What else have you learned using mostly your eyes? (eg reading, recognising faces)

As they give their answers, indicate with your finger on the board where you would write the words.

What have you learned that you couldn't have learned without using your bodies, your hands and legs? (eg writing, cycling)

What else have you learned using your bodies, touch and movement? (eg all sports, cooking, dancing)

What have you learned that you couldn't have learned without using your ears? (eg tunes of songs)

What else have you learned because you could use your ears? (eg speaking, listening to explanations and instructions)

Give each child a copy of the mind map and ask them to work in groups of two, three or four to decide what words they want to write on the lines. Not everyone in the group has to write the same words, but they will remember more things between them than they would working alone.

Ask the children to share their mind maps in groups of three or four.

The senses

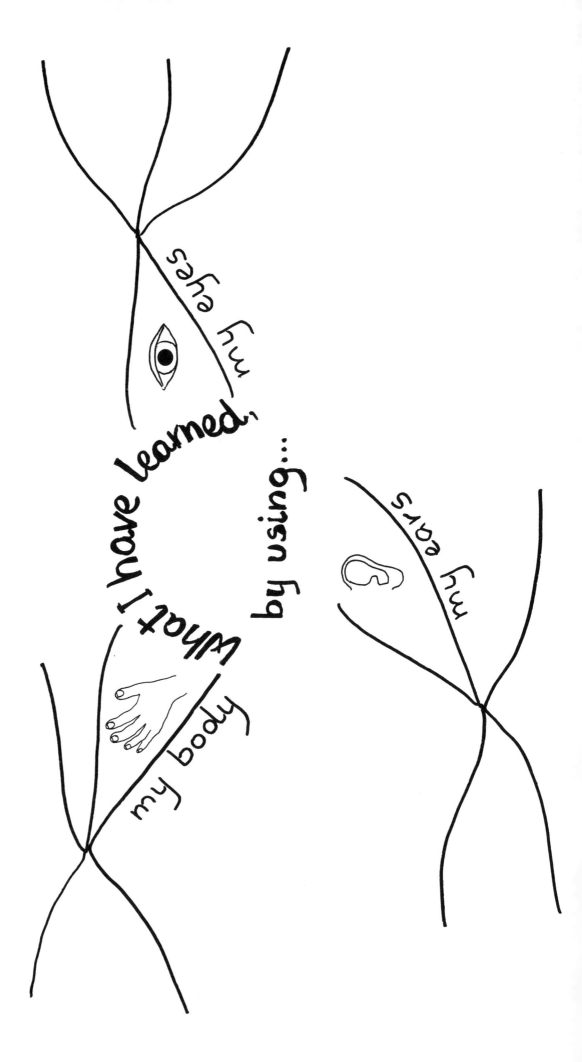

What I have learned, by using...

my eyes

my ears

my body

STEP THREE

Lesson 15: *Time for compliments*

Why do it? To teach children to focus on the positive, to see good in other
people and to be able to accept compliments with grace and appreciation

What you need A big space on the classroom wall, children's photographs, a
scrapbook for every child, writing paper and pens

Time 10-45 minutes

There are several activities which can be done at different times. You may engage the
whole class in the activities or focus on just one or two children at a time.

Tell children that paying compliments is telling people what we like,
admire and appreciate about them. Not only are many people not used to
paying compliments, many find it difficult to receive compliments.

Partners

Tell children to sit opposite a partner.

Look at your partner for a while and think, 'What is it that I like about
you?' 'What do I like about the way you look?' 'What do I like about the
kind of person you are?'

Write what you appreciate about your partner on a sheet of paper.

Say to your partner: What I like and appreciate about you is (read
everything you have written on your piece of paper).

Your partner's job is to sit and listen.

Then give your partner the sheet of paper to keep.

Now swap and let your partner tell you what he or she likes and
appreciates about you while you listen and accept the compliments.

Circle

Have one child sit in the middle of a circle of children. Tell the group to
think for a moment about all the things they like and appreciate about the
child in the middle.

Ask all children to write their comments and then tell the child in the
middle what they have written.

Collect all the sheets of paper and give them to the child to put in his or
her scrapbook.

Building Self-Esteem

Photographs

Give each child their photograph and ask them to stick it in the middle of a sheet of blank paper. If you don't have easy access to photographs, children can draw pictures of themselves and write their name underneath, but photographs are much more powerful.

Children exchange sheets. They think about the child in the picture and write around the photograph what they like and appreciate.

Display the sheets on the wall for everyone to see and enjoy. After a week children glue their sheets in their scrapbooks.

Receiving applause

Talk with children about how it makes them feel to be complimented and whether they enjoy receiving compliments. It is not easy for everybody to accept and enjoy compliments!

Give everyone (including yourself) the opportunity to receive and accept applause. Teach them first how to bow and curtsey. Then ask them to imagine that they are famous pop stars or that they have just won the world cup for football and ask them to show you how they would react – without touching anyone else. (Jumping up and down, waving their arms or punching their fists up high, etc.)

Everyone stands in a circle. Ask for a volunteer to start, or indicate a child you think will cope well with the experience. Tell them that all they have to do is to accept and show their appreciation, maybe by smiling and bowing or waving. Say everyone will have a turn to be in the middle.

Tell everyone else to clap and cheer as much as they can. Indicate children to go in and out relatively quickly and keep the circle clapping and cheering. If anyone seems particularly nervous, let them go in at the same time as a friend. Make sure you take your turn too.

Lesson 16: *Listening with your heart*

> ***Why do it?*** Only when we really listen, can we begin to truly understand other people; listening is one of the most crucial skills in developing EI
>
> ***What you need*** Enough copies of the hearts sheet (p54) for everyone to have one or two hearts
>
> ***Time*** 15 minutes

Tell children that listening is not as easy as it seems. To listen we need to do two things:
- stop talking
- clear our minds of the chatter that goes on inside our heads.

Ask children to say or write down three things people often do when they only pretend to be listening, eg while they're on the phone. (Read emails, watch TV, think about something else, think about what they're going to say, keep interrupting with what **they** want to say.) Explain that when we truly listen and give someone our full attention it can feel as if we're listening with our heart instead of with our ears.

Give everyone one or two copy/copies of a heart to colour in and cut out.

Ask everyone to think of something interesting that has happened to them – maybe at home or on holiday or when they were a baby – or that happened to someone in their family, or things they enjoy most or what they want to do in the future. (Give lots of suggestions to prompt children to think of something.)

When half the class has thought of something, they each find a partner and in their pairs the children sit or stand together away from others, where people can't hear them.

Listeners hold their heart over their real heart, slightly to the left of centre in their chest. Alternatively they hold two hearts behind their ears – which is more fun but has more potential for silliness. (Just asking children to hold their hand over their heart can also be very effective.)

Remind listeners that what they have to do is really listen without speaking. The speakers then tell their stories.

Stepping Stones ©*Eva Hoffman and Susan Norman 2004*

Developing Emotional Intelligence

After about five minutes, ask speakers how it felt to be listened to. Did they feel noticed, appreciated, valued?

Ask listeners what it was like to listen in this way. Was it easy? Did they keep wanting to interrupt and say something? Were they able to concentrate on the speaker's story?

Repeat the activity with children swapping roles.

Again discuss with the children how easy or difficult it was to listen – and to speak. Older children can write down how it feels to really listen and to really be listened to.

Uncurling your ears

This simple activity gets children ready for listening at any time. It works by stimulating acupressure points.

Demonstrate as you explain to children what to do.

Take hold of the top of your right ear with the first finger and thumb of your right hand. Massage around the outside of the ear, moving from the top down to the earlobe, as if you were uncurling your ear outwards.

Do the same with the left ear and the left hand – and then do both ears together.

Ask children if they can hear more clearly.

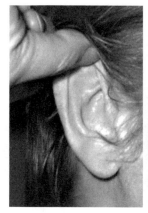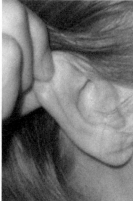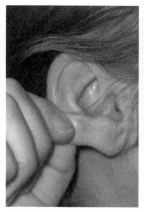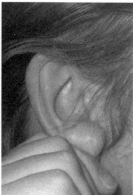

54

Thinking creatively with Mind Mapping

Lesson 17: *Connecting new to old*

Why do it? To find out what children already know about a subject so that
new information can be connected to existing knowledge

What you need Coloured pens or markers, one copy of the 'Electricity mind
map' (p56) for each child, and blank paper for the follow up

Time 30 minutes

Give children a copy of the 'Electricity mind map'. Ask them to write key
words on the thick branches to represent whatever comes to their minds in
connection with the topic. If they have more information which is
associated with any of the first ideas, they should write it on the connected
thin branches.

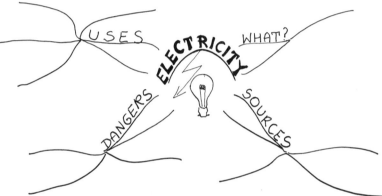

Encourage children to
share their work with
others and add to their
mind maps by taking
some ideas from others
and giving some of
their ideas in return.

Tell them that when they learn new things about the topic, they can add
them in a different colour. They add new thick branches for new ideas, and
thinner branches for ideas connected to something they've already written.

New topics

Next time you are teaching a new topic, use the same approach. Give
children a blank sheet of paper (or a copy of the 'Dotty mind map' (p15),
possibly adding additional main branches to represent each sub-topic you
want to introduce. Ask children to draw a picture representing the topic in
the centre of the page.

Ask children to write key words which come to their minds when they think
of the topic, one on each branch. Or give them mind maps with the sub-
topics already filled in and ask them to write or draw on the smaller lines
any ideas or pictures that come to mind when they think of the words on
the branches.

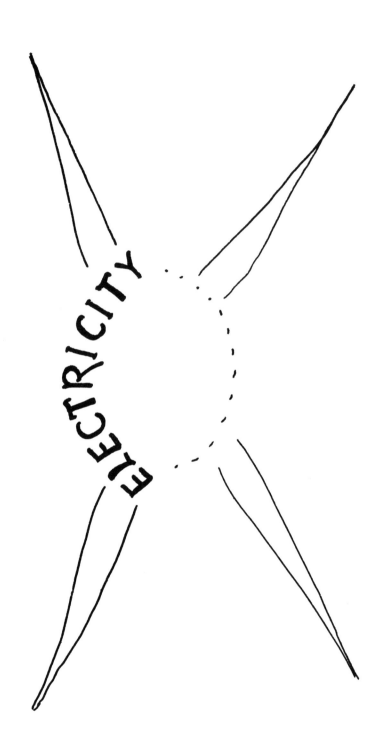

Moving to enhance Learning

Lesson 18: *Crossed wrists and ankles*

Why do it? To connect the right and left hemispheres of the brain, to focus
attention and calm down the brain/body system
What you need Space to move, water for each child
Time 5 minutes

Encourage children to drink water regularly throughout the day and
always before doing integration exercises.

Instructions for younger children (or children with balance difficulties)

* Sit in your chair with both feet on the floor.
* Put your left hand on your right shoulder and your right
  hand on your left shoulder.
* Cross your ankles keeping both feet on the floor (if the
  right hand is on top, the right leg needs to be on top and
  the other way round).
* As you breathe in, press your tongue to the roof of your
  mouth; as you breathe out, relax your tongue. Breathe like
  this a few times more.
* Uncross your wrists and ankles.
* Put your fingertips together in front of your chest and
  breathe normally three times, in ... out ... in ... out ...
  in ... out.

Instructions for older children (See photos on next page)

* Stand up straight and take a deep breath in ... and out.
* Stretch your arms in front of you and turn your hands so that the
  backs are together, with thumbs pointing down.
* Cross one hand over the other, so palms are facing and thumbs are
  still down.
* Interlock fingers and thumbs.
* Turn your locked fingers downwards and inwards and rest your
  interlocked hands (now facing up) on your chest.
* Cross your ankles.
* As you breathe in, press your tongue to the roof of your mouth; as you
  breathe out, relax your tongue. Breathe like this a few times more.
* Untangle yourself and put your fingertips together in front of your
  chest. Breathe slowly in ... out ... in ... out ... in ... out.

Calming sequence

Children now have all the information they need to be able to calm themselves down when they feel stress. When something unpleasant has happened to them, making themselves feel better is a much more useful response than fighting or running away. It is also a very useful sequence to practise regularly to get them into a good state for learning – and to do just before they sit down to take a test.

- Have a drink of water.
- Put your hand on your heart; take a deep breath in through your nose and very slowly breathe out through your mouth.
- Sit or stand in the crossed-wrists-and-ankles position.
- Breathe in through your nose with your tongue pressed to the roof of your mouth, and then relax your tongue as you breathe out very slowly. Repeat three or four times.
- Untangle yourself, put your fingertips together and continue breathing slowly and regularly until your heart beats normally and the stress melts away. Enjoy the feeling of calm strength.

Stepping Stones ©*Eva Hoffman and Susan Norman 2004*

Discovering your Amazing Brain

Lesson 19: *Brain buttons*

Why do it? To wake up the brain
What you need Water for every child
Time 2 minutes

Stimulate your brain buttons (yourself or with the children) at any time you (or they) are feeling a bit sleepy and need to wake up.

First find your brain buttons. They are situated on either side of your breast bone, just below your collar bones. They're easier to find if you hunch your shoulders forwards. When you rub them strongly with the tips of your thumb and middle finger, these points can often feel a bit tender. (If they're tender, then you NEED this exercise.)

People are different, so on some people they will be quite far apart and on others relatively close together. Basically, they will be just under the end of each collar bone. (Brain buttons are actually acupressure points which stimulate the brain.)

Drink water before you start.

The exercise is to place your thumb and your middle finger on your two brain buttons, and to place your other hand over your tummy button.

Sit or stand straight and gently massage your brain buttons for about 30 seconds.

Swap hands and continue massaging the brain buttons for another 30 seconds.

Lesson 20: *The intelligences wheel*

> *Why do it?* To have each child celebrate their strengths and see they are valued
> *What you need* A large sheet of paper or cardboard, tags or stickers with children's names/photographs, glue
> *Time* 15 minutes (plus time to prepare the wheel)

Make a large circle (on flip chart size paper) and divide it into eight segments. In each segment write in large print the names of the individual intelligences: Music, Picture, Practical, Words, Nature, Numbers, Body and Emotions. In order to have eight segments, combine Self and People intelligences as Emotions.

Ask children to look back at or remember their intelligences mind maps from Lessons 6 and 13.

Give each child, or ask them to make, a sticker or tag which represents them – either their name, their photo, or their own named drawing of themselves. Each child chooses their strongest intelligence and attaches their tag to the appropriate segment. Every child then chooses their second strongest intelligence and writes their name in that segment in the colour of their choice.

In this particular activity, for purposes of raising all children's self-esteem, ensure that all children have the same number of entries on the wheel.

Display the wheel for a week.

Talk with children about the rich mix of intelligences in their class and how important they all are.

Graph

Ask older children to make a graph showing the distribution of intelligences in the class.

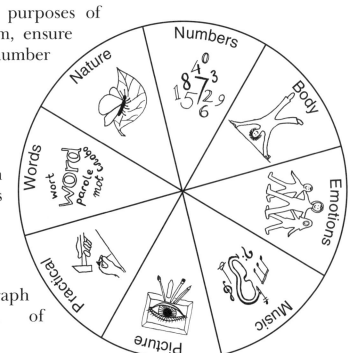

Using your Senses for Learning

Lesson 21: *How I like to learn*

> *Why do it?* To awaken children's awareness of ways of using their senses for learning
>
> *What you need* A copy of the 'How I like to learn' handout (p63) for each child
>
> *Time* 30 minutes

Tell children that we like to use different senses for learning and some of us like to learn in different ways from others. This activity is about helping them know how they like to learn best.

Give a copy of the 'How I like to learn' handout to each child. As you read out the statements written on the sheet, ask children to draw a smiling mouth, a sad mouth or a neutral mouth to show whether they like this way of learning. They should only put a smiley mouth for the things they really like doing, not those they do because they have to.

Tell children that how they like to learn now may be different from how they liked to learn in the past, and that their preferred ways of learning may change again in the future. But it's useful to know how they like to learn now. The statements may give them some ideas about different ways of learning they can try. The more ways you can learn, the easier it is to learn.

All answers are valid and good.

Ask children to share their answers with two or three other children. Do they like to learn in the same way? Or have they given different answers?

Example lessons (with older children)

Ask the children to think of an example of a lesson in school in the last two weeks when they have learnt something in the way they like learning. And then something in the way they do not like learning. Ask them to tell their partner.

Ask them to think with their partner if there is anything they (not the teacher) could do to make their learning easier now they know some of the possibilities. Anyone who has a good idea can tell the whole class.

Using your Senses for Learning

Statements 1, 4 and 7 refer to Kinaesthetic learning

Statements 2, 5 and 8 refer to Auditory learning

Statements 3, 6 and 9 refer to Visual learning.

This activity is not about labelling children as 'visuals' or 'kinaesthetic learners', etc. It is to raise awareness that people like to learn in different ways and to help children find the ways they like to learn best. If you notice that some children have a very strong preference for one way of learning, keep an eye on them and make sure that they get enough exposure to this kind of learning, particularly when you are dealing with new material.

Finally, make sure you know how YOU like to learn best. This will be the way you tend to teach 'naturally'. Children who learn in the same way as you will tend to do well in your class. Remember to include styles of teaching which help all different kinds of learners.

Stepping Stones ©*Eva Hoffman and Susan Norman 2004*

How I like to learn

Draw a smiley mouth for everything you like to do when you're learning. Only draw a smiley mouth for things you REALLY like to do, not the ones you do because you have to.
Draw a sad mouth for everything you don't like to do.
Draw this mouth if you don't like it or dislike it.

1 I like to make things with my hands and learn about them.

2 I like to listen to people telling me things I need to know.

3 I like to read for myself what I need to know.

4 I like to move when I am learning; it helps me remember things and it helps me think

5 I like silence when I am trying to concentrate.

6 I like to see pictures; pictures help me remember things better.

7 I like to learn by visiting places and experiencing what I need to learn.

8 I like to close my eyes to hear things better.

9 I like to see people when they are speaking so that I can hear them well.

Remember, **we are all different, unique and special.**

Further information

If you want to continue your exploration of Accelerated Learning, we recommend the following books and sources of information:

The Learning Adventure by Eva Hoffman (Learn to Learn 1999) *Many more activities similar to those in this book to use with children.*

A Guide to The Learning Adventure by Eva Hoffman (Learn to Learn 1999) *Exercises and suggestions on using an Accelerated Learning approach, plus some background information.*

Introducing Children to... series by Eva Hoffman (Learn to Learn 2001-2) *Photocopiable books of lessons to use directly with children aged 7-12.*

 Introducing Children to their Amazing Brains

 Introducing Children to their Multiple Intelligences

 Introducing Children to their Senses

 Introducing Children to Mind Mapping

Transforming Learning – Introducing SEAL Approaches compiled by Susan Norman (Saffire Press 2003) *Introduction to all aspects of Accelerated Learning with sources of further information, for teachers and trainers.*

The ALPS Approach by Alistair Smith and Nicola Call (Network Educational Press 1999) *Introduction to all aspects of implementing an Accelerated Learning approach in primary schools.*

Brain Gym and ***Brain Gym: Teacher's Edition*** by Paul Dennison and Gail Dennison (Edu-Kinesthetics Inc 1989) *Illustrations and simple instructions for doing Brain Gym exercises with children – teacher's edition gives teaching tips and background information.*

Smart Moves – why learning is not all in the head by Carla Hannaford (Great Ocean Publishers 1995) *Information about the body's role in learning and how the two hemispheres of the brain work together – with a chapter on Brain Gym.*

Teaching for Success – the brain-friendly revolution in action by Mark Fletcher (Brain Friendly Publications 2000) *Practical AL teaching ideas.*

www.seal.org.uk SEAL (Society for Effective Affective Learning) – *the leading-edge learning organisation which promotes AL through its publications and transformational conferences.*

Introducing the latest materials from Eva Hoffman and Susan Norman

inspiring teaching

A six-part feast of everything you need for In-Service
Training in Accelerated Learning with your staff:

- **How Children Learn**
- **Self-Esteem and Emotional Intelligence**
- **Movement and Learning**
- **Amazing Brains**
- **Motivation**
- **Multiple Intelligences and Sensory Learning**

www.inspiringteaching.com   www.saffirepress.co.uk
